To: Matthew

DOGGIE IN A DIAPER

A True Story

By Phil and Lisa Sichhart

Illustrations by Dan Cooper

♡ CoCo Pierre

AuthorHouse™ LLC
1663 Liberty Drive
Bloomington, IN 47403
www.authorhouse.com
Phone: 1-800-839-8640

© 2013 Phil and Lisa Sichhart. All Rights Reserved.

No part of this book may be reproduced, stored in a retrieval system,
or transmitted by any means without the written permission of the author.

Published by AuthorHouse 07/08/2013

ISBN: 978-1-4817-6569-5 (sc)
978-1-4817-6570-1 (e)

Library of Congress Control Number: 2013911112

Inspired by Coco Pierre with the help of Phil and Lisa Sichhart

Any people depicted in stock imagery provided by Thinkstock are models,
and such images are being used for illustrative purposes only.
Certain stock imagery © Thinkstock.

Because of the dynamic nature of the Internet, any web addresses or links contained in this book may have changed since publication and may no longer be valid. The views expressed in this work are solely those of the author and do not necessarily reflect the views of the publisher, and the publisher hereby disclaims any responsibility for them.

For all the unwanted animals.

Coco Pierre is a special doggie....but most people do not know why.

Coco barks like other dogs...

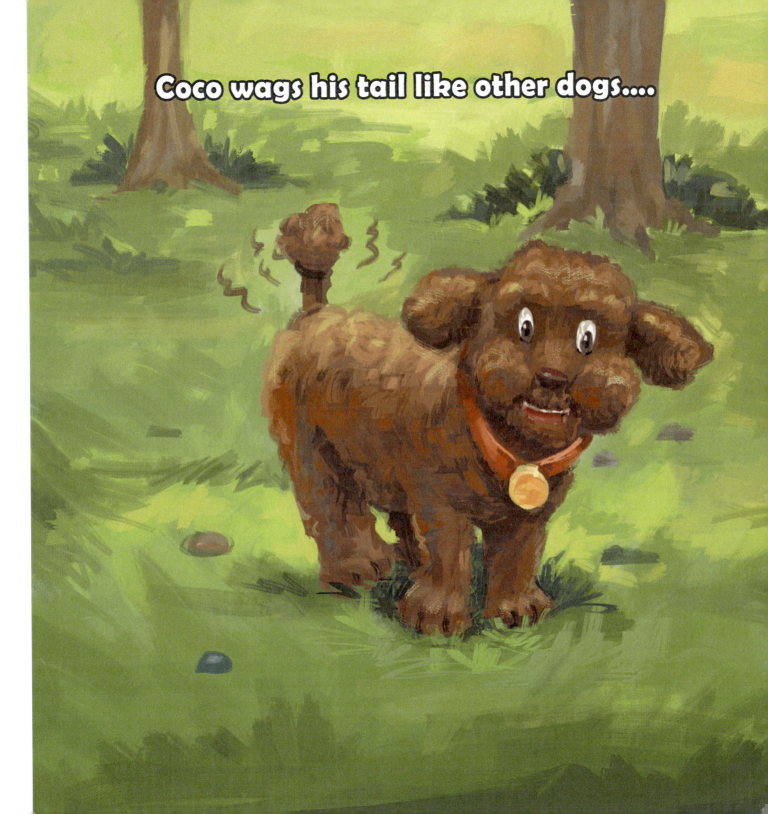

So, what makes Coco so special?
This is his story...

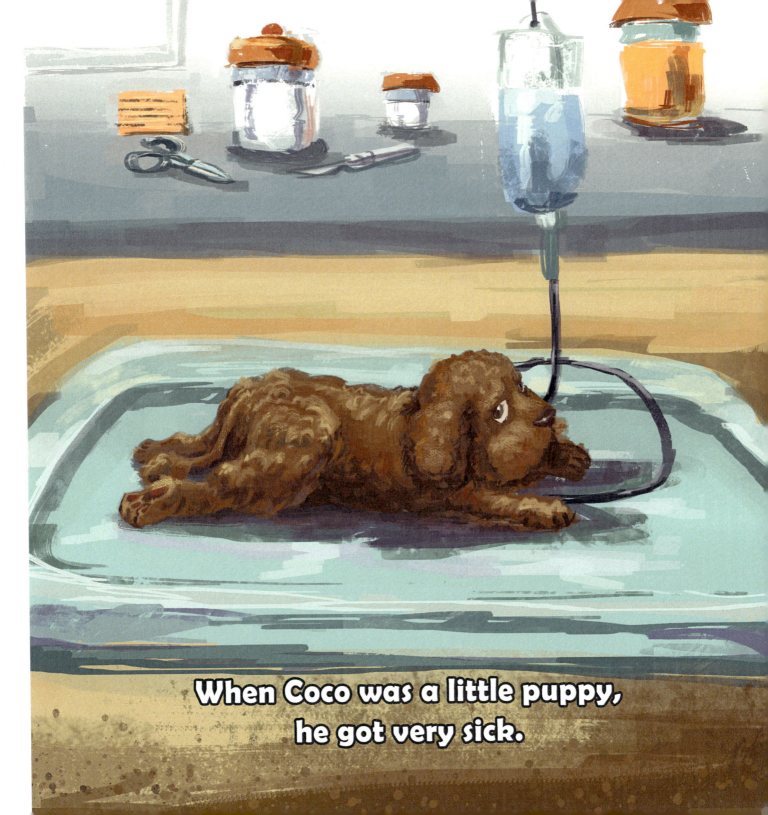

The doggie doctors, called veterinarians, made Coco better!

But, he would always be different from other dogs..

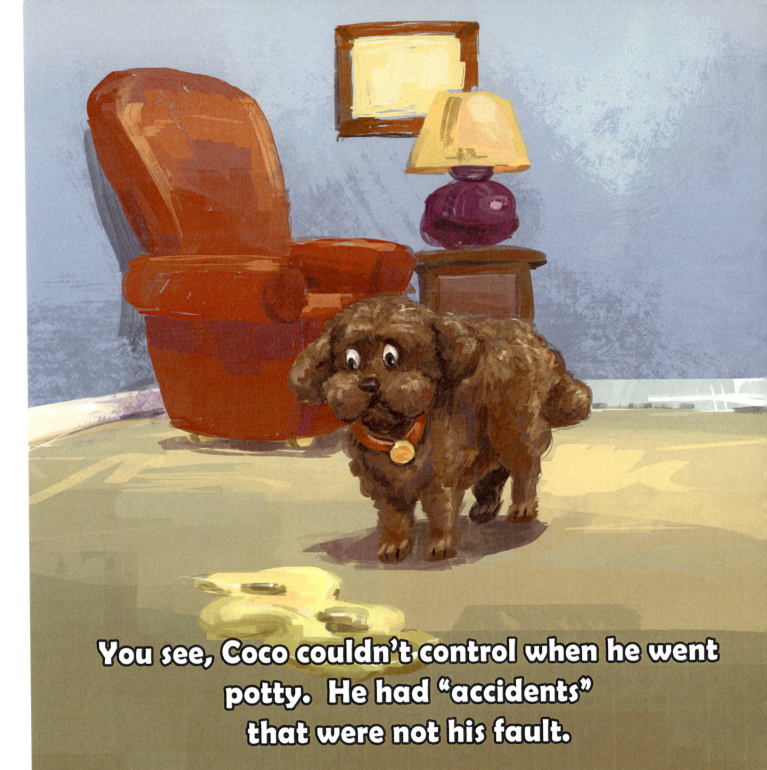

You see, Coco couldn't control when he went potty. He had "accidents" that were not his fault.

Coco's family was happy he was better, but did not have time to take care of his special needs or clean up after his accidents.

Lucky for Coco, a rescue group took him from the shelter to a foster home. There, Coco would wait to be adopted.

Coco liked playing with his new friends at the foster home, but he was a little sad that his special needs meant that he had to stay in a cage or outside. He longed to have a family and sit on their laps!

Many families came to meet Coco since he was so cute. Sadly, the families did not adopt him because they did not want to take care of his special needs or clean up his accidents.

Then one day, a couple came to see Coco. They did not mind that he had special needs and knew that they wanted to adopt him into their family.

It was important to Coco's forever family that he did not have to live outside or stay in a cage. So, they thought and thought until they had an idea….

When human babies have potty accidents, what do their moms and dads do about that?

So, Coco got special diapers that fit dogs. Now, he could go ANYWHERE as long as he had his new parents to change his diaper.

Now he could play in the house and sleep in bed with his forever family!

He had diapers for Summer....

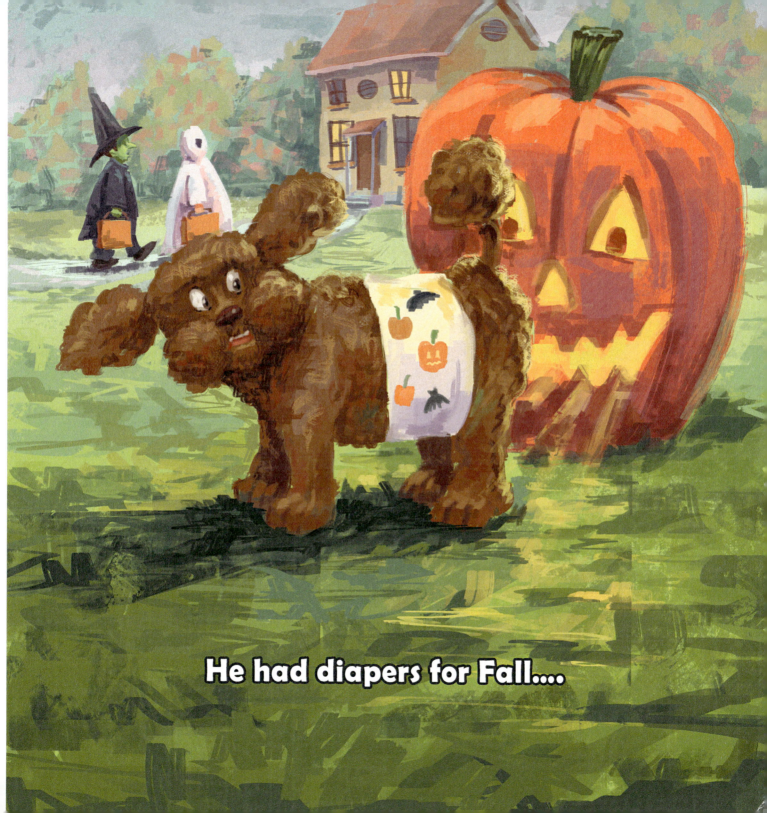

He had diapers for Fall....

But his favorite diapers of all were his everyday diapers, because for Coco, every day was now a happy day with his forever family who only saw the "special" in his special needs.

Made in the USA
San Bernardino, CA
18 April 2018